RILYN'S REVELATIONS

Wisdom of a Five-Year-Old

By

Cheryl Gore Pollard

Rilyn's Revelations: Wisdom of a Five-Year-Old
2015 by Cheryl Gore Pollard
All rights reserved

PUBLISHED BY Dogtrot Publishers
w/ CreateSpace.com

also available in an eBook publication

All rights reserved. No part may be reproduced without written permission from Cheryl Gore Pollard, author.
Characters may or may not have had name changes. This book or parts thereof may not be reproduced in any form, stored in a retrieval system, or transmitted in any form by any means without prior written permission of Cheryl Gore Pollard, except as provided by United States of America copyright law.

Cover Photo/arrangement: Cheryl Gore Pollard Illustrations: Greer Ellen-Elizabeth Harper, Rilyn Virginia Harper, Carly Reese Archer, and Ellie Wren Archer.

Interior formatting and cover design: Eleos Press (www.eleospress.com)

ISBN-13: 978-0692440452
ISBN-10: 0692440453

PRINTED IN THE UNITED STATES OF AMERICA

Illustrated by
Greer Ellen-Elizabeth Harper
Rilyn Virginia Harper
Carly Reese Archer
Ellie Wren Archer

Dear Readers

Rilyn is the fourth in our line of seven grandchildren, ranging in age from thirteen to seven months. She's five, six in April, hitting square in the middle of the crew—three older and three younger. All my grandchildren are special, and all have wonderful gifts. But this is about Rilyn and the way she—just is.

Rilyn has the gift of conversation, and she keeps her gift in its prime. She never stops chatting. She talks or sings when we're traveling and when we're working in the flower or vegetable gardens. She carries on private conversations with her dolls or toys, keeps a lively dialogue going with her siblings and cousins during playtime, and even talks in her sleep.

I think, when describing her, of Mrs. Beatrice Huckeba. My friend, Hazel (Beatrice) Reeves, often spoke of her grandmother, Beatrice Huckeba—also Hazel's namesake. Hazel was quick to say how her grandfather fondly recalled his wife's ability to converse. "Her tongue is hinged in the middle and flaps on both ends," he'd say. That attribute has been reflected in Hazel's manner of speech, too. It would be easy to say that Rilyn could be Beatrice the Third.

Rilyn speaks freely and often with an innocence of the young that is unusual for a five-year-old. Her out-of-the-box remarks bring laughter and joy that lift every occasion and bring smiles to all who hear. As I began my collection of

Rilyn's 'profound' statements, I discovered lessons for a Godly life are buried in them, and began examining her whimsical remarks and uncovering priceless jewels hidden there.

I hope you enjoy her stories and think about how we can use them to further the kingdom of God and spread love for all his children.

Cheryl

To a great husband, grandparents everywhere,
children and grandchildren of all ages,
and good friends.

Table of Contents

Dear Readers... i
Silver Strands... 1
Coolin' Off.. 5
Vowels and Consonants 11
It is MY Time!.. 17
Long Distance Love... 23
Eat More Gourds.. 27
Watch Where You Step.. 35
A Little Planning Goes a Long Way........................ 41
Let's Par-Taay!... 47
Reading, Set, Go!.. 53
Step into the Light... 57
Good Summer Veggies 63
More Than a Flower Pot Filler................................ 69
Smooching, Smooching... 77
When Ya Gotta' Go, Ya Gotta' Go.......................... 83
Hip Hop.. 89
Goin' Through the Motions 95
Can't Those Girls Leave My Nativity Alone? 101
Acknowledgements 111
Other Books by Cheryl Gore Pollard..................... 115

Silver Strands

After years of using color to cover the gray in my hair, I decided to forego the chore of coloring and let the gray become me. I kept my hair short, used lighter colors with each new application, and finally was color-free. I was a different-looking G-Mama with my white hair rather than my usual brown, but so much time could be saved, and so much easier for me to get going; wash, fluff, and head out.

"Is that your natural color?" I often heard. "It's such a pretty shade."

One day as Rilyn and I were grocery shopping, we met a friend whom I'd not seen for several months. My hair transformation was a real shock to her, and she remarked on the change much as others had. She added, "I wish I could let my hair go gray, and I would if it was the lovely color yours is—not brassy or dull."

For once, Rilyn was quiet while my friend and I spoke. She stood listening and absorbed every word.

As my friend and I parted and Rilyn and I resumed our shopping, she looked up and said, "G-Mama, don't worry, you're not old, you're just blonde."

My spirits were instantly lifted. Oh Rilyn, I thought, I may have felt that I'm old, and I may be the gray-haired lady, but you're right; I'm not old. I am blonde.

Cheryl Gore Pollard

≈

For as he thinketh in his heart, so is he:
Proverbs 23:7

≈

Many times this scripture has been taught, preached, and expounded upon, but usually in the context such as right and wrong, evil and good, sin and Godliness or greed and giving. It seems that Rilyn's gem of an axiom that she said in the grocery store could steer toward the kind of attitude we have. "As we are in our hearts."

Times of difficulty are always present in our lives: illnesses, finances, family disconnect or problems, stress, jobs, relationships, and on and on, like a sad, gray rain cloud hovering over our heads and threatening to drench us in even more misery. The answer to coping, and possibly solving our problems, lies in the attitude we adopt.

How are we dealing with our 'gray' to turn it to 'blonde'? After all, supposedly, blondes do have more fun.

Do we look for the good, the positive possibilities that lie hidden in our personal turmoil? Those little joys like finding a lost coin that has been sitting in the bottom of our purse all along, or discovering the first blooming daffodil, or listening to the little one telling about losing the first baby tooth. Simple little joys.

Do we consciously look for things that are hidden blessings? Or do we simply close our minds and moan and bemoan our situation?

Attitudes do not come automatically imbedded in us at birth. We adopt much of how we view and respond to our world: bright positive or gray negative.

Many of our mindsets are learned from mom and dad, some come from relationships with our friends, and others grow in us as a result of how we want to be perceived, but may somehow get twisted around. If people have ideas of being accepted in a positive manner and that satisfaction is not met, they think that negative attention is better than none at all, and their actions—actions without thoughts of consequences, spiral toward negativity. When they 'wake up' and realize that they are looking at themselves and the world through gray lenses, it is time to change their ways and clean up. And it is not easy.

Just as any bad habit is hard to break, the habit of having a negative or bad attitude is hard to break. Following a few simple steps will allow us to snap the links in our bad habit chain. First we must realize that we must identify the gray side of our thoughts, and only then can we objectively examine them and make better choices. Then we can consciously work to quit the gray and see our blonde side. A good attitude begins growing every time we stop and think about how we are going to respond to events or actions. Blonde slowly begins taking over the gray. Our vision becomes clearer. Our hearts become happy hearts. Big, beautiful, sparkly red hearts like the best of hearts on the prettiest valentine. The effort to change how we look at and perceive the incidents in our lives is worth every bit of sweat and determination we put into it. Living with a positive, happy heart beats dragging through the gray doldrums any day. Becoming blonde is truly a labor of love.

Go for it! Have a Happy Heart as you discover the joy in having a super-blonde attitude!

Cheryl Gore Pollard

Coolin' Off

Summertime is the time when we love to cool off in the backyard pool. We keep all sizes of swimsuits on hand in a special cabinet in the basement so when the 'Grands' come on weekends, they know exactly where to go and can quickly change from their play clothes to their 'swimsoops' and cool off in the sparkling, cool water.

One Friday afternoon after gathering the crew for their weekly Friday night sleepover and arriving home, I watched as they poured out of the car and descended to the basement like a troop of wild monkeys to find their swimsuits, yank them on and get ready to hit the water. I heard the children's excited voices as they dug through the pile of swimsuits to find his or her favorite.

I stood in the kitchen stirring a fresh pitcher of sweet tea and listened as three girls and two boys sped up the stairs and watched as they dashed out the door, colorful towels flapping over their shoulders like wings of tropical birds. Then, a few minutes later, here came Rilyn trailing behind, clomping her bare feet, padding across the floor. She stopped in front of me, (naked from the waist up) put her hands on her hips, cocked her head to one side and asked, "G-Mama, I found the bottom to my tankini, but do you know where I might find the lid that goes with it?"

Hiding a grin, I took her hand. She had only half of what she needed and to be completely dressed for her swim; she needed the top to her tankini. Together we headed to the basement to plow through the scattered swimsuits to, hopefully, find her lid.

≈

*And ye are complete in him which is the
head of all principality and power.
Colossians 2:10
and
Howbeit I believed not the words until I came, and mine eyes had seen it, and behold the half was not told me. Thy wisdom and prosperity exceeded what I heard.
1 Kings 10:7*

≈

How many times have we begun a project and found that we had only half what we needed to complete it? Started a cake or casserole and realized we only had part of the ingredients? Or watched a television show for it to "be continued" and knew without a doubt that we'd never remember to watch the following episode and find out how it ended?

There are countless people, too, who do not know the complete story of Jesus. It is a saddened state of mind to think about our neighbors, friends, and family members who have heard about Jesus, but have only gotten half the story. Sure, they know who Jesus is, know He is Lord, but they have not found the 'lid' to seal their story of salvation.

There are those who have learned enough about Jesus's purpose to realize something is missing from their lives. They feel the void, the emptiness. They have reached the point of 'digging through' the scriptures and praying, searching for whatever they realized they are lacking. Those are the lucky ones, because they realize that somewhere there is a lid that will seal their spiritual void and make them whole. And it is within their reach!

The unfortunate ones are those who are living their lives like that jumbled pile of swimsuits lying limp in our basement: no desire or perceived need to search for the other half of the story of God's filling love. They do not realize they do not have a lid—that they need to be filled.

This is where we who have found our lids and are complete and whole in our relationship with Christ have a responsibility. First, we pray for ourselves so that what we do and say will be at the appointed time, and that our words are exactly what Christ would have us say to those poor souls. Then our duty is to take the seekers, the searchers, those half-filled friends' hands, pray with and for them, support them, and guide them through their search. They will find just what they had been searching for: the very things that fits best and what is just right for them. They, too, will be filled, completed, and become whole in Christ.

It takes more patience and love for us to help those who are spiritually blind to the Holy Spirit, those who are wandering aimlessly through their everyday routine, perfectly content to stumble along, walking in darkness. Our job becomes harder as we help lead them to fullness; our lives must shout out Jesus's love so that they will see Him in us and yearn for the happiness and love that shines from our fullness within. The Holy Spirit will speak to their hearts, and then we can take their hands (as God has sent the Holy Spirit and their hearts have been softened) and help them find and experience God's all-compassing, complete, filling love.

Together we come to know and share the love that God has for us and gives to us through Jesus's resurrection, and fills us with the Holy Spirit. His grace will exceed all that we have seen and heard.

Both the 'empties' and the half-filled will find their lids and become complete and whole—from bottom to top. And their faces will be filled with smiles just as wide as Rilyn's was—when she and I found her 'lid'. And like her too, they will run with joy and anticipation to join their brothers and sisters and cousins (in Christ) as they share their special times together.

Ah, what a day!

RILYN'S REVELATIONS

Vowels and Consonants

With Rilyn having a sister and two brothers, and all of them going in different directions throughout the day, after dinner is family time to wind down and enjoy some laid-back time together.

One night they were in the den, Rilyn snuggled beside her mother in her big chair (that particular night it was with her mom; sometimes dad got lucky) and they were watching a popular television show where the contestants guess letters of the alphabet until they solve the phrase and win a prize. One young lady was having a particularly hard time guessing letters in the puzzle, having no luck filling the blanks. Rilyn looked up at her mom and said, "That lady's not so smart; she's not getting any of the letters right."

Ginger explained that the lady must be pretty smart because she had to audition and be really good just to be chosen as a contestant.

Rilyn accepted the explanation and settled back to watch the remainder of the show. They watched as another contestant began filling in space after space. Rilyn was impressed. Again, she looked up at her mom and pointed her finger at the TV. "*That* girl is really good! She must have gone through kindergarten and first grade TWICE!" she exclaimed.

"What do you mean?" my daughter asked, somewhat befuddled.

"Well," Rilyn stated, "kindergarten and first grade is where you learn your letters, and she sure knows hers good!"

My daughter smiled and looked over at Rilyn's dad who was sitting across the room, eavesdropping on their conversation.

Chuck just grinned and shook his head.

≈

Study to shew thyself approved unto God . . .
2 Timothy 2:15

≈

Rilyn hit the mark again.

In order for us to show ourselves approved to God, we must have a firm foundation on which to build. Just as learning our letters and numbers when we are young provides us the building blocks we need to succeed later in our lives, our studies in the Bible teach us the necessary building blocks we need to become knowledgeable ministers and witnesses to share God's word.

We all realize, as we pass through our day-to-day living, that learning is an ongoing process. No matter how mature and 'learned' we are, we discover new things every day. As we age, it is our responsibility to pass the love for learning about God along to our children, and also to the 'new' children of God we adopt into our church family—no matter their age.

When our children are very young, we teach them in short and simple ways: bedtime prayers and blessings for our food. These are their first conversations with God. The simple, childlike prayers continue to grow and, hopefully, mature into a lifelong habit of having daily talks with God.

As our toddlers grow and mature, they love listening to and learning through Bible stories. Especially those rousing and rebelling ones found in the Old Testament. The very same ones that I remember reading aloud as my young son and daughter sat still and listened, breathlessly, so intently, as I read.

As youngsters attend Sunday School, Vacation Bible School, home study time, and especially their time at G-Mama and Granddaddy's, they hear about heroes found in exciting stories: Jonah getting spewed out of the whale's mouth, Moses being rescued from his reed 'boat' by a princess, or Shadrach, Meshach, and Abednego in the fiery furnace, the Hebrew people walking on dry ground through the sea, David slaying the giant, and so many more. Accounts like these whet young learners' appetites for more storytelling. As the fascinating stories are learned, and our children grow and begin to read on their own, they begin searching for more stories in the Bible . . . and they learn about Jesus's life as they read. On to the New Testament . . .

A miraculous birth in Bethlehem, a blind man suddenly able to see, a despised tax collector forgiven, even a man called Lazarus, dead! And Jesus, with little effort, brought life to him again. Even in song, children learn—"Zacchaeus was a wee little man"—and Jesus loved him, just as it is sung in my children's favorite, "Jesus Loves Me." They listen and come to realize just how much Jesus loves them when they hear about his ultimate sacrifice as he suffered on the cross, and find that Easter isn't about a bunny and eggs, it is celebrating our Lord's resurrection—providing for our 'happily ever after' as we will live forever in such a beautiful place.

Then during their middle and teen years, they also learn by watching our lives (Godly examples), to search the Bible and find Godly lessons which will guide them and support them through every experience they face. Knowledge that will lead them to salvation.

No matter what our age, we must study and learn, so we will gain knowledge and share God's grace and love.

As Rilyn says, we need to build our spiritual foundations as sturdy as we can: get our A, B, C's, down pat. And sometimes we need to look at them more than once to be sure we have 'learned good'.

And then pass our wonderful knowledge on to gain the priceless prize—everlasting life.

RILYN'S REVELATIONS

1 2 3 4 5 6 7
A B C D E F G
H I J K L M N O
P Q R S T U V W X
Y Z 8 9 10

It is MY Time!

This past summer has been as long as a double-jointed snake and hot as a July firecracker. Not only has it been long and hot, but also extra busy. It seemed that everything that needed to be done was crammed into three short months' summer break. In the middle of this, Rilyn's mom and dad, Ginger and Chuck, planned to take the family on a quick get-away to the beach for some down time. As usual, Ginger promised to give me a quick call to say 'all is well, and we arrived safely'.

To make her summer even more stressful, Ginger had recently enrolled in a local university to earn an additional educational degree. On Friday night, the night before leaving for the trip, she worked the entire night on one of her research papers. It was required to be sent via computer to her professor on Saturday at the preassigned time. When she was sure her assignment was finished and shipshape, she saved it on a flash drive to submit it to her professor from her laptop at the beach condo. Needless to say, due to the time spent researching and typing her papers and projects, Rilyn's 'Mom time' had been severely cut into, and she was more than tired of Ginger's time on the laptop. This vacation was, to Rilyn, an expected and welcomed retreat and some one-on-one with her mother.

The Saturday morning they arrived at the condo everyone was busy as hens in a henhouse: checking in and unpacking, getting food into six hungry stomachs, and settling in. All the while, Ginger watched the clock so not to miss the deadline getting her assignment sent to her professor.

Ginger's promised call came later that night after all the items on her 'to do' list had been checked off.

"Sorry the call is so late," she said, "We are here, and thankfully everything has settled down. We're getting ready for bed, and my paper is turned in! I think we can really enjoy our time from here on out." We chatted another few minutes, and before disconnecting, she started chuckling and wanted to tell me about Rilyn's latest.

"Guess what Rilyn's said this time," Ginger asked.

"I can't imagine," I answered.

"You know how she still gets her 'time' words mixed up? This afternoon when I got out the laptop to send my paper, she was right beside me. She didn't like that I was setting up to work. She gave me one of her frowns, and I knew she was going to let me have it. In her say-so voice, and shaking that little finger at me, she said, 'Mama, if you get on that computer now, you <u>cannot</u> get on it yesterday!'"

Ginger hardly got the last words out, she was laughing so hard. "I wish you could have heard her," she added.

Yep, I thought, I wish I could have, too.

≈

For we are but of yesterday and know nothing,
because our days on this earth are but a shadow.
Job 8:9
and
And he said unto them,
Go ye into all the world, and preach the gospel to every creature. He that believeth and is baptized shall be saved; but he that believeth not shall be damned.
John 13:35

I am probably the world's most productive and successful procrastinator. I assume there will be a tomorrow (unless Christ's return comes first), and often change my plans from today's to tomorrow's. And more often than not, when tomorrow comes, how I wish I had completed my plans yesterday. I find numerous reasons to extend some particular chore until the next day, and then tomorrow is here and so is the job—waiting. I have not accomplished anything (or very little) of what I had planned to do. And that time was lost. I know all about the old saying, "Don't put off 'til tomorrow what you can do today," but hardly do I heed it. Whoever made that statement was a very wise person.

How many times have I meant to send a card to a sick friend, a lonely shut-in, a friend in grief? and wandered on to another project to do something else. Later I realize that I had not put one thing in the mail. My moment had passed. My thoughts turn to what I had done yesterday, and many of the things I had done were good things, but I had neglected the most important ones.

Often too, I wish I could go back in time and 'fix' something I had done or change something I had said. What was done was done, and I cannot go back. What I can do, however, is work to help heal any wounds that I have made. The hurt will always be there, both for me and that of the person I wronged, but the effort I put forward to make amends will never be wasted.

We are of today: yesterday has passed leaving only memories. We can learn from those, but should not live or dwell in them. It is a sad thing that there *are* those people who experience pain and guilt daily—in the present, harboring sorrowful memories and thoughts from yesterdays and cannot get beyond them. Those sad yesterdays keep those people from realizing the happiness and joy of today and anticipating joys of tomorrow.

It is pertinent to remember: today is a new day and tomorrow can be better. For sure, to paraphrase what Rilyn so aptly said, we'll not get back to work yesterday.

Our mission is to work today: go into the world! Tell about Jesus!

Faith comes by hearing, and for sure if we did not tell anyone about Jesus yesterday, we must busy ourselves to get the job done today. Putting off today's message until tomorrow will not guarantee that the message will be told. Today is our day to speak.

Our days on this earth are but a shadow, and we should make the very most of today's time. Time past cannot be recalled. We know nothing of tomorrow, but with faith and a good dose of grace, we have the strength to look ahead and seek better days. Sure, we live in shadows of yesterday, but they are only shadows. We live in God's time, and it will not be long before we walk out of this shadow and into the light of our everlasting life—no more yesterdays and no more tomorrows—simply the glorious jubilation of today with Him in our Heavenly home.

Yes, like Rilyn, be happy today and fill the hours spending time with our family and communing with God. Our spirits will be lifted and our conscience clear, knowing that we have accomplished even more than what we'd made plans to do yesterday.

Long Distance Love

Usually Granddaddy and I join the Harper family on at least one family vacation, and we all head to the beach. This past summer we passed on their invitation to go along on their second, short vacation to Florida and stayed home. Granddaddy Jimmy had had knee replacement and was still on the mend. I had my flower and vegetable gardens to tend. As always, Ginger and I spoke on the phone before they left, and she promised to call in to let me know of their safe arrival.

When she checked in, she filled me in with their activities and upcoming plans and then, just as she was ready to hang up the phone, she said, "Hold on, Rilyn wants to talk to you."

"Oh, boy!" I thought. "She misses me already." I was anxious to hear her voice and let her know how I missed her, too. I heard jostling and static noises as the phone was being transferred from Ginger to Rilyn.

"Hello, G-Mama," she said.

"Hi, Rilyn," I responded.

"G-Mama," she drawled. "How are the fig trees doing?"

What! Well, not the words I anticipated at all! I struggled to get my thoughts straight. I was all ready to respond to her voice with something like, "I miss you, too!," and so I had to scramble to think of an appropriate reply. I searched for words to answer her unexpected question.

"You know," I quickly improvised, "the winter was bad this year and the fig bushes were all killed back to the ground. They're putting up new branches, but I'm afraid we won't have any figs this year . . . maybe next year, though."

Through the phone all I heard was this low and disappointed, "Awwww." We finished our little talk in comfortable short chat mode, ended our conversation and smooched a phone kiss before disconnecting.

Then I thought: What about those fig trees?

≈

Abide in me, and I in you. As the branch cannot bear fruit of itself, except it abide in the vine, no more can ye except ye abide in me.
John 1:8

≈

Rilyn, same as a couple of her cousins, loves picking and eating juicy sweet figs right off the bush. We have several fruit-bearing producers growing around our house. Scuppernong vines, cherry and apple trees, blueberry bushes, and fig bushes are all that we can manage to squeeze on our small acreage. All the Grands enjoy searching for, picking, and eating whatever fruit is in season, but only Rilyn and her cousins, Carly and Ellie, partake of the figs.

Part of the joy of the hunt to get ripe fruit is climbing up in the huge bush and searching behind the large green leaves to find the brown fruit hanging, waiting to be picked. Squealing in delight when one is found, it is quickly picked and pulled apart and popped into their mouths right there. "Mmmmm," I hear as the girls bite into the sweet fig's flesh. When they have somewhat satisfied their taste buds there at the bush, they fill their hands with fruit and return to the porch steps to sit, eat, and share their harvest.

If the bush becomes diseased or, like the past winter, gets killed back to the ground due to the harsh cold, it cannot bear fruit. It just does not have the maturity, health, or nutrients to make little figs. So it is in our lives.

Sin is the disease that attacks our life-vine and prevents us from producing fruit, so we must rid ourselves of sin. We must keep God alive in us. For without Him, we cannot bear any fruit at all.

Fruits are gifts that God has ordained especially for us according to our abilities and capabilities. I can imagine them, lying dormant deep within our hearts, wishing they could burst out and grow, ripen, and be expended so that, in turn, our lives will be enriched and nourished. Having God abiding in us and, as we abide in Him, giving us grace enough to keep sin at bay. Our fruit can grow and mature, grow within us and 'pop out'. As our fruits ripen, people see them working in us and being shared to help others, and they want some of the good stuff, too. By sharing God's gifts, we spread seeds and some will mature and the fruits born there be harvested.

I ponder Rilyn's question: How are the figs doing? And I ask, How are OUR figs doing? Are they maturing, growing sweet and firm and spreading seeds? I surely hope so. Just like my fig bushes that now have new shoots sprouting from the ground and reaching upward, we should continually strive to be renewed and looking upward to God our Heavenly Father, ever ready to bear good fruit.

Eat More Gourds

Around our place here on Dogtrot Farm, everyone loves summertime. The good weather and extra daylight provide opportunities for Grands to spend more time with us and help out with chores—the outside ones they think to be fun instead of labor. My enjoyment comes from watching and listening as they work alongside me, visiting PaPa Gore and Dara (great-grandparents), watching butterflies and newborn goats and calves, digging worms and going fishing, and among lots of other adventures, turning the soil and planting.

One morning Rilyn and I were readying a few rows in the garden to transplant tomato plants from seed trays into the warm ground. Days before, Granddaddy had plowed the soil and had laid the furrows straight. We gathered our hoe, fertilizer, and tomato plants, and walked across the yard to the garden spot.

Lo and behold! Right next to the rows where we were going to set the tomato plants some other young green plants had sprouted.

"G-Mama, what are those?" Rilyn asked as she peered at the little shoots.

"I think they're gourd plants," I replied. "Look behind you up on that pole in the yard," I instructed. "See the gourds Granddaddy cleaned out and painted? He cut a hole in each one and hung them high. He put them up for the Purple Martins, beautiful birds who come and visit every year. They raise their babies in the gourds and fly and circle, chatting cheerfully to each other. They grab and eat flying insects as they soar, and that helps us not have so many pesky 'skeeter bites. Granddaddy must have left a few seeds inside some gourds when he cleaned them. The mamma bird must have picked them up and dropped them here when she began building her nest—she likes a good, clean house for her babies."

Rilyn's gaze meandered from the gourd pole to the new plants growing, peeping from the ground at our feet like miniature green flags. I could almost see the thoughts whizzing around in her head, imagining the birds flying out of the white gourds and dropping the seeds where they'd landed and sprouted.

"Let's dig them up and move them along the fence," I suggested. "They will reach out long vines, like arms, and cling to the fence, and new gourds will grow and hang from them. We might have some new birdhouses for granddaddy to work on this winter."

Her eyes lit up like Christmas sparklers. We searched the workshed and found an old tablespoon and tin pie plate and returned to the tender gourd plants.

"Hold the pan while I dig," I instructed. I scooped up several plants with the old spoon and lightly laid them in the pan Rilyn was holding. All the while excitement echoed from her words as we gathered up the plants. "How long will it take to see the gourds? Will the cows in the pasture eat the vines growing on the fence?" And oodles of other questions spilled from her lips like water from a pump.

"Come on, let's get them planted so we can finish the tomatoes," I said.

Reaching the fence, I knelt and dug a shallow hole in the ground along the fence. "Hand me a plant," I instructed, and Rilyn balanced the pan in the crook of her arm and gently plucked a plant from the pan and gave it to me. We continued down the fence line, chatting as we placed the gourd plants in their holes and patted the dirt smooth around each one.

"This one has lots of dirt on the bottom of it," Rilyn remarked as she shook the plant to remove part of the soil from its root.

"No, don't do that!" I said. "Leave as much dirt on the roots as you can. The plants need the soil to protect their roots so they can grow healthy. Their tiny roots are delicate and if they get smushed, the plant might die."

"Okay, G-Mama." She said. And she then worked diligently and patiently to handle the remaining plants carefully and protect their tiny, fragile roots.

At last we had transplanted the gourds and made our way back to the garden to work on the tomatoes. "I can hardly wait to see our new gourds! I bet that Mama Martin will love her new house that's going to grow on the fence," my little farmer said as she grabbed the hoe and began chopping a hole in the garden soil, getting ready to plant our tomatoes.

Oh, I know Mama Martin will certainly love that house, I thought.

≈

> *But when the sun was up, it was scorched; and*
> *because it had no root,*
> *it withered away.*
> *Mark 4:6*

≈

The movie, *Roots*, became a hit and created a frenzy of interest across the nation as people began to search for their 'roots'. Where did we come from? What is our ancestry and cultural heritage? Glovis, my cousin, is one of those who can manipulate the computer so easily and find her way around search engines—she's one of the best. She began digging into our family history and researched the family far, far back. She discovered our 'old' roots reached across the big pond to later become transplanted deep in southern soil. She uncovered some interesting facts and characters, a few dubious ones, and even a couple of absolute surprises—that should be kept under our hats to keep our ancestral lineage respectable.

Jesus taught through the parable of the sower of seeds in Matthew 13. A farmer went out to sow his field. He scattered his seed by hand and tossed them out as he walked. He had prepared a spot, but as he tossed his seeds, no matter how carefully he aimed for them to land on his tended soil, some went astray.

Hungry birds watched, and when seeds bounced and twirled into the edge of the field, the birds flew down and gobbled them up.

Gone.

Some of the seeds fell in safer places and the birds did not get them. They sprouted and began sending out roots, but they had landed on stony ground, a place where they could not be properly nourished and grow. They did not have enough soil for their roots to reach down and anchor, to drink and obtain nourishment. They withered away when the hot, scorching sun came up.

Gone.

Still other seeds managed to form roots, send them down, and began growing! But they, too, found themselves in a bad place: they were among thorns—and those seeds' roots were no match for the big, bad thorny roots. Oh, those little plants tried, but the thorns bullied and choked them dry.

Gone.

Yet there was hope. Many of the farmer's seeds fell on good, fertile ground that he had plowed and tended. They were able to send down roots, grow strong, and produce a good bounty. Some brought forth hundreds more seeds, some less, but they all grew and added to the harvest.

The farmer was there all the while. He sent out his seeds with the knowledge that all of them had potential to grow and bear fruit. Many fell in places that either were dangerous or did not have the support, nourishment, and protection they needed to survive. The farmer had to stand and watch helplessly as some of his precious plants failed to thrive. Their roots were not strong enough to sustain them. Imagine his disappointment in his realization that he would reap less than one-hundred percent growth and maturity of all his seeds—his hard work wasn't to pay off as he had hoped.

How hard he had worked! All the preparations he had made so that he would have a great harvest seemed in vain. Imagine, too, our pastors who plan, prepare, preach and teach their hearts out, and we, his congregation, do not give **our** one-hundred percent. We can do better.

God, our Father, feels disappointment when He watches and hopes that we, as His 'seeds' will grow and thrive, but we often fail to mature and become productive. We can do better.

Thankfully, we are mobile, not like the stationary seeds that must lie where they fall. We are blessed with good minds and the ability to make decisions, natural attributes we can use to change many life situations for the better, and we can physically move into a position where we can find good soil and dig our roots in.

We have resources to help us grow: our church friends, those little whispers from God, prayer, Bible study. But we must be careful and watchful and not suddenly find ourselves in dry, stony places, places that are separated from the goodness and grace of God. We cannot grow strong roots and thrive in those places. We must be careful to remove ourselves from groups of thorns who will pull at us and choke us until we separate ourselves from God. Like the seeds—gone.

Just as Rilyn tenderly handled the fragile plants and tried so hard to keep the new roots covered in soil and planted firmly in rich soil, we not only have the responsibility to keep ourselves nourished and form strong roots, but to support and feed the young plants that are beginning their Christian growth in our fields. The stronger our roots, the better we can serve God and bear wonderful fruits fit for His dinner table.

You should have seen and heard the chatter as Rilyn and her cousins walked the fence line the following fall and gathered gourds in the fresh, cool air. Like the farmer in Matthew, not all our plants survived, but most did, and we gathered our harvest. All twenty-seven gourds. Each a different size, each a little different shape, but all beautiful, sturdy, future homes for the Martins. Ready to do the job that was planned for them to do.

RILYN'S REVELATIONS

Watch Where You Step

Our log home is situated right between two large pastures. In the south, fire ants love pastures. When the nests get so big and the weather is right, queens emerge and fly away like tiny winged fairies, only to drop back onto the ground and build new nests. I think 99 percent of the queens from the pastures decide to drop into our yard to raise their families—right along beside us. It is a constant battle, fighting fire ants and keeping our yard free of the stinging, hurtful pests.

One Friday afternoon after the Grands finished swimming and all but Rilyn had dried off and returned to the house for a sweet snack, she and I noticed a giant fire ant bed beside the concrete around the back of the pool.

"Come on, Rilyn, we gotta get the fire ant poison and put some on this nest," I said, heading to the shed to get the poison to sprinkle on the ant bed. "If those fire ants get on you and bite you, they will set you on fire! You'll know for sure why they're named 'fire' ants."

We hurried to the shed and returned with the yellow granules, and I began sprinkling them around and on the huge nest. Millions of ants emerged, crawling and tumbling over each other in great surges like black waves crashing and tumbling on the beach, trying to find and bite any intruder and protect their home.

Rilyn asked question after question: "What is that stuff you're putting on it? Why are you sprinkling it there?"

I explained that the ants would gather the granules and carry them deep down into their underground tunnels and burrows and eventually eat them. When they did, they would die.

With the final words—they will die—Rilyn suddenly lifted her face to me and I saw terror streaking and shooting through her wide brown eyes. She pulled up her shoulders and spread her arms wide and whimpered, "But G-Mama, don't they know?"

≈

My children are destroyed for lack of knowledge, because thou hast rejected knowledge, I will also reject thee.
Hosea 4:6

Tell ye your children of it, and let your children tell their children, and their children another generation.
Joel 1:3

≈

Such profound implications in three little words: "Don't they know?"

Both my grandmothers were wives of Methodist ministers. That is where the major resemblance between them ends, however. Mom's mom, MaMa Sheets, was lively and funny. I see her in my mind's eye laughing and 'carrying on'. When I think of her, I see a wide, toothy grin and shining eyes. Her cheeks bobbed higher when she laughed and caused the skin surrounding her eyes to become all crinkly. Her hands also played along with her joy. She would clap them together and often slap her knees in glee whenever a funny story was shared. She was a delightful, Godly woman.

My dad's mother, MaMa Gore, was more serene, a reader, and an extremely modest person. I can picture her quiet smile after she heard a funny story, more often than not, when she was really tickled, she pressed her lips together to form a tight, happy line running across her face. Her happy smile was usually followed by her hastily reaching to pull the hem of her dress further down over her knees, just to keep her hands busy, I suppose.

I remember one time when I finally persuaded her to go to the mall with my sisters and me, but she did not shop, preferring to sit in the huge atrium and be a "people watcher," observing folks as they scurried through the various shops like squirrels gathering nuts. She explained how she would notice different individuals as they did their window shopping or hurried along burdened with packages. She said as she focused on a person, she would think of a possible name for them; imagine what occupation they might have, and what hobbies they would enjoy. She would create a whole life for them. She wondered, too, if they were saved by the blood of Christ. She wondered if 'they knew'.

Both lovely grandmothers are now with God. During their time here on Earth, both were concerned about telling others the Good News. They lived lives that impressed everyone they came in contact with *To Know.* Through their words and deeds, they taught us not to accept the enticing sinful poison fed to us by Satan that can only end in spiritual death.

Chris, the son of Ronald, one of my high school classmates, is a missionary who witnesses and teaches in Malaysia. He and his family came and spoke at our church, and he told a fact that amazed and disturbed me greatly. According to him, there are more than half the people in this world who do not know Christ as their personal Savior. To those of us who have been 'raised' in the church, that is an astounding statement.

Why don't they know? Haven't they been told? Why are they still crawling and tumbling through this world in ignorance? Why don't they heed the message if they have heard?

We are all missionaries, those who are ordained by Christ to tell others the Good News. Often people do not know about God's grace simply because **we** have not told them—personally told them. People who work with us, who might carpool or ride the bus with us; people who are part of our community organizations; and people who are parents of our children's friends. We should help them To Know.

More importantly are the people in our families—our closest loved ones. Surely we cannot sit idly and watch as they partake of the poison—sin. We must find ways to let them know.

As parents, it is one of our greatest responsibilities to teach our children about God's saving grace—lead them through our words and actions to know about Jesus and salvation. We cannot leave this obligation to anyone else—it is ours to teach our children to pray and seek God so they will become children of His. I want to be sure that someday we will all be singing praises to God together in Glory. It will be too late then to ask ourselves why our loved ones are not with us in Heaven.

Didn't they know?

RILYN'S REVELATIONS

A Little Planning Goes a Long Way

Miss Clarice was a lovely, kind ninety-two-year-old lady who attended our church for many, many years. Her husband and son had long passed, and her nearest relatives, two nieces, lived a distance away. Miss Clarice continued living alone in our community and until she reached ninety, was able to drive to church, to the local fast food restaurant and pick up her daily early morning biscuit, and get to her hairdresser on Thursdays. When her eyesight failed, she continued driving as long as she could, and refused—somewhat stubbornly—not to give up the wheel without a fight. Finally she had to give in. My husband and I picked her up for Sunday services, and she relied on certain ones of us at church to chauffeur her to the doctor and get her 'hair done'. She had to forgo her morning biscuit, however.

Rilyn sometimes rode along with me when I drove Miss Clarice to her hair appointment, and on some Sunday mornings after a Saturday spend-the-night, Rilyn was with us on the ride to church, so Miss Clarice was a special friend to Rilyn, too.

One Thursday when I went to pick up Miss Clarice for her hair appointment, she could not get her out of bed. I called an ambulance and she was hospitalized. When she returned home, Jane, a special friend, came to stay and help with daily chores and meals. Then it became necessary for home health to visit and help, too.

Eventually, Miss Clarice, not without kicking and complaining, went to live in an assisted living facility, where a few months later she died peacefully in her sleep.

Rilyn, knowing Miss Clarice, and of course having chatted often with her, and visited Miss Clarice in her 'new home,' understood when she passed away. Her little ears were on high alert as she listened while some of us reminisced, laughed, and cried over this wonderful lady's life. During our conversation, we mentioned how unfortunate it was that her relatives lived so far away and were unable to visit regularly and play a more important role in her life. And how fortunate we were to have been so close to her and shared blessed time with her.

A few weeks later, after getting our Friday night chicken nuggets for the Grands, we rode along on the way home, catching up on the past week's highs and lows. Out of the blue, Rilyn brought up the subject of Miss Clarice. She was obviously concerned and bothered that Miss Clarice had no children to care for her and see to her needs in her last years. As we talked and the conversation was finally coming to an end, she shrugged her shoulders and offered her final opinion of the situation. "Well," she said, "You know if you don't have any when you're young, you won't have any when you're old."

It took me a minute to digest her words. "Yep," I replied, "You're right about that." And we drove quietly on home.

*Laying up in store for themselves a good foundation
against the time to come,
that they may lay hold on eternal life.*
1 Timothy 6:19

. . . I go to prepare a place for you.
John 14:2

≈

In the days that followed, Rilyn's words stuck with me. I thought of friends who, for some unknown reason, never were able to have children. They are blessed with nieces or nephews that love them and will step in as they are needed. I thought of different cultures, and how care of many parents rest solely on the shoulders of their children as their parents age, and the senior's needs change from independence to dependence. Thankfully, most children, whatever culture, step up to the plate and care for their aging parents.

Then the idea of 'not having any' broadened in my mind. As a retiree, I am more than aware of what my husband and I need to keep our household going in our golden years. Our children are wonderful; our grandchildren are super, and we were fortunate to have thought ahead in our younger days so that our retirement can be lived in comfort.

There are things that couples starting out should think about while they are still young, so that when they get old, they will be prepared and 'have some'.

1. Health, both spiritual and physical. Do not wait to have healthy spiritual health. Study, attend church, pray, and serve others. Keep Godly thoughts. Build a strong spiritual foundation and when the time comes for greater hope and faith, it will be there.

Maintain a healthy physical body and mind. Our bodies are temples, and God's temples should remain clean. Restrain from unhealthy lifestyles, especially alcohol and drugs. Try to maintain a healthy diet and exercise the body, just as you exercise the mind.

2. Home. Decide whether to spend your last days in a home of your own—town or country, or in an apartment with upkeep included. Having someone available to maintain house and grounds is essential when age burdens our bodies too great and prevents us from getting out-and-about. Set aside a little every month to help cover the cost of retirement living.

3. Money. Plan for retirement. As hard as it may be to set a little back or make investments during early years that should pay off later, do so. Too many people reach the age of retirement but have to continue working because they have not managed to pay off their major creditors.

4. Stay away from credit cards as much as possible. Owing money to this type of creditor has the potential to bury you in debt. Retirement will be a long time coming with misuse of credit.

5. Make sure you have a place prepared. Jesus has prepared the final place. And it will be the perfect place.

Just as Rilyn so aptly said, if you don't have any when you're young, you won't have any when you're old. Work hard while you're young so that when you're old, those years will truly be the Golden Years—years when you will reap the rewards of early planning and preparations. Years to spend with those you love—family or not. Years to laugh and enjoy the wonderful family of God.

Cheryl Gore Pollard

Let's Par-Taay!

*I*t was Big Ed's birthday, and the Harper family was on their way to visit Chuck's mom, Tanya, and his step-dad, Ed, where they would celebrate Ed's birthday dinner. Somehow Ed had earned the name Big Ed, and that's what he's fondly called. He's as good as gold and the kids were excited to go celebrate his special day with him.

During the short drive, Rilyn peppered her parents with questions: "How old is Big Ed? What did we get him for his birthday present? Will we have balloons or a jumpy house (a large inflatable for kids to play in) and, Do you think our party treats will be good?"

Ginger explained that this birthday party was for Big Ed, not one of her friends, and there would only be a good dinner and cake, no party treats or special playtime.

Rilyn slumped back in her seat with a pouty mouth and wrinkled, frowny brow. Ginger heard her mumble, "I don't know why old people don't have fun parties."

Ginger peeked over at Chuck and he returned her gaze. He just kept on driving.

≈

Make a joyful noise unto God, all ye lands; Sing forth the honor of his name; make his praise glorious.
Psalm 66:1

Poor Rilyn, thinking that only the young folks have fun parties. The birthday parties she was accustomed to usually took place at the park, or playground, maybe the water park where they could swim, at the honoree's pool, or just a good ole' home party with games and fun. Today's custom is that each attendee leaves with a bag full of candy and treats—a kind of 'thank you' for coming and joining the birthday girl's or boy's celebration. So no wonder she was disappointed when she found out that no such was happening at Big Ed's party.

She did get ME to thinking about what she'd said about old people not having fun times, party or not. I pondered that idea and wondered if her thinking, as such, had any merit. Did she not see us old folks having any fun? We can make a joyful noise as loud as anyone. Hills and mountains are really old, and King David proclaimed how they did their share of singing and celebrating with joy!

Rilyn didn't know it yet, but as she grew and matured, she would realize that the idea of fun would evolve as she her body and spirit did. Fun for one isn't necessarily fun for all:

Hayden's idea of fun is building computers and working his way through a maze of obstacles to win the game. And learning about all sorts of odd and unusual facts.

Greyson has fun in sports—especially baseball, and skiing. He loves spending time with his friends and loves that special time hitting the slopes with his dad.

Greer is the social butterfly, and her idea of fun is, well, socializing. She loves to dance, and she has a special talent at becoming whatever character she is playing in her acting class. She is most believable as that shy pioneer, inquisitive Santa elf named *Jingles*, or a pink fairy godmother.

Rilyn's fun comes spending time with others too, along with letting her imagination fly as high and fast as her words and thoughts can carry her.

Carly has fun with her art and spending time with her cousins. She has fun swimming and climbing trees, and can utter some pretty good words of wisdom herself—but that's another story.

Ellie, Ellie just has fun! She IS fun! She skips and runs wherever she goes, and when she spies an animal is the only time she slows down. Cats, dogs, donkeys, or goats, she's going to pet, feed, kiss, and coo sweet sayings to them.

Isabelle isn't old enough to know what fun really is, but she laughs and smiles a lot, and right now has her fun as she walks, climbs, and pokes into cabinets. She shares her expression of fun every time she spies Granddaddy or me—her eyes sparkle and her few teeth shine through her wide grin as she runs, with her arms held high, for us to scoop her up and smother her with kisses.

Each and all have fun spending time outdoors, reading, and painting or drawing wonderful pictures.

I have fun doing all that, too!

Just because we continue to climb up in years, doesn't mean we stop having fun—we have fun in our own way; safe, comfortable, and super enjoyable. That's not to say that we don't sometimes just break out and let go to have fun in new and different ways. We do! Last New Year's Eve, Becky and Richard, (friends who are mine and Jimmy's age) danced well into the New Year. They glided and pranced until the wee hours of the morning. Becky said she never felt tired at all, as if she could have danced until the sun came up!

I remember a time in my early teens when daddy had nailed a basketball ring high up on the side of an oak tree in our back yard. A couple of boys came over, (not dating boys, 'brother' kind of boys), and we decided to have a basketball game. We were one player short, and mama said she would join in. Wow! Unbelievable!

At that time, I thought my Mama was sitting on top of the hill and ready to get on over, too old to play basketball. I must admit. She got around pretty good. It was a fun afternoon.

Whatever our age, we really don't have to have jumpy houses, balloons, or treat bags. Like in Psalms, no matter how old we are, we can always make a joyful noise and praise God. And Rilyn found that out just how much fun, young and old can have, as they celebrated at Big Ed's birthday party that night.

So yes, Rilyn, old people can have fun, too.

RILYN'S REVELATIONS

Reading, Set, Go!

Rilyn, like her siblings, loves school. She has been so excited learning her alphabet and numbers and during her prekindergarten year she learned the sounds associated with the letters. She has begun sounding out words and that has really 'set her on fire,' as her mom often says, to sound out more words.

One Friday afternoon as the Magnificent Seven and I turned onto our long drive off the main road and guided the car along the long trail through the pasture where we live, I gave permission to the Grands to unbuckle their seatbelts. They love to lower the car windows and look out at the cows and calves as we slowly bump along the long gravel drive to the house.

Rilyn quickly unbuckled and crawled from the back and perched on the console beside me. Chattering away, her quick eyes surveyed the dash, asking questions about this button and that. Suddenly her eyes stopped on a particular spot and her lips slowly began moving. "G-Mama," she asked, pointing to one of the buttons. "Does that say re- reset?" she asked.

I glanced at the button and smiled. "You're getting really good!" I exclaimed. "That says reset all right. Just think. Pre-K and you're already reading!"

"What does the reset button do?" she asked.

"It means that when you push it, the settings automatically go back to whatever setting was first set up before someone set new ones."

"Oh," she replied, satisfied with my answer.

She sat back and beamed. Her moment of quiet satisfaction did not last long. The gate to the yard swung open and we pulled in. As Granddaddy met us, all of her reading—and the reset button was quickly pushed to the back of her mind as the crew piled out of the car, laughing and gathering their backpacks to spend the night with G-Mama and Granddaddy.

≈

Create in me a clean heart, O God; And renew a right spirit within me.
Psalm 51:10

≈

That night, after Greyson was settled in his bed, Hayden still bumping around upstairs getting ready to settle down, the girls all giggled out and asleep beside me, and Granddaddy collapsed in the extra bed in the basement, I thought about Rilyn and the reset button. How, during many times in our lives, we need to stop and think about how far we have come, what our everyday routine has migrated into, and whether or not we can (or should) keep up the pace.

Unfortunately, today's lifestyle does not leave much time for quiet meditation and reflections. We are in a rush and hurry to get to the next place while our minds are racing along planning the *following* event. Our calendars are full and often chocked with more than one place and time to be on any given day. And that is in addition to the eight-to-five that fills many working days! Even retirement—the 'easy living' time—is spent checking appointments, trying to work in time to go to the doctor, watch Grands' ball games, dance recitals, plays, partake in their school activities and participate in local clubs and charities. Not to forget church activities—

Whew! Too bad our lives do not come with a huge automatic RESET button.

As we scramble through our days, we almost become living in a zombie-like trance: legs move, eyes read, TV remote gets plenty of use, dishwasher filled, clothes washed, doctor met, prescription filled, to bed, get up, and start all over.

At what point do we realize just how far into left field we have let our lives become? There comes a poignant burst, a flash in our brains, that "Huh?" moment, when time stops and our life zooms into focus. We realize we have to stop and press that reset button and get back to a calmer, simpler time. That takes some planning.

With the realization that our days are coming and going and passing in a long blur, we know it is time to stop and reevaluate our schedule. Reset.

Set priorities so that we can live happier, more stress free with each coming day. Reset.

Think, evaluate, plan, and cut out what we do not need and maintain time to meditate in prayer and thanksgiving. Reset.

Share God's love and presence in our lives, and experience joy in the things we choose to keep. Reset.

Take a deep breath, hit that reset button, live life and not miss any joy, and sit back and be proud. You will be glad you did.

Cheryl Gore Pollard

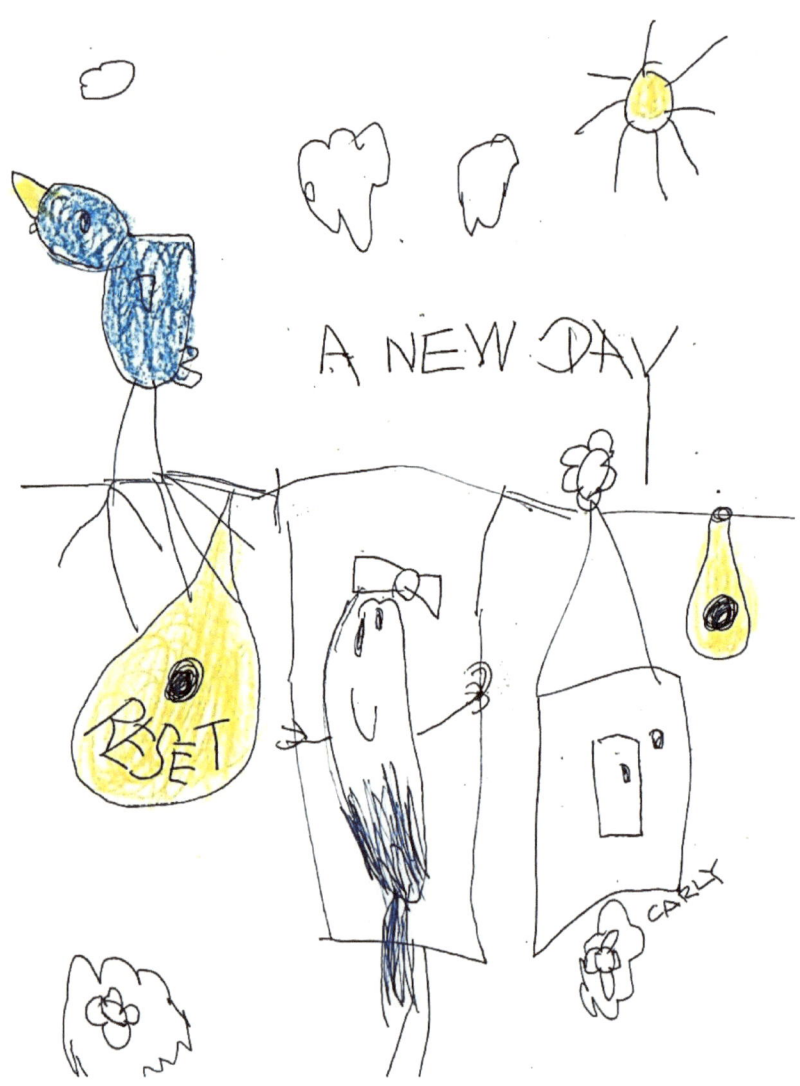

Step into the Light

*E*ven with a king-sized bed, Friday nights become a challenge when four girls—ages three to eleven—plus me, try to find a spot between the covers to sleep. And with the space beside G-Mama the prime spot, little ones often become whiny and demanding after an afternoon of heavy playtime, and argue about who is going to sleep beside me.

Greer, the oldest, usually grabs the edge of the bed and hangs on like a spider in her web. She is happy to have her usual spot as she forms a 'wall' between the floor and top of the mattress, so I don't worry about the little ones falling off and hitting the floor from that side of the bed.

Then it is a sparring match between Rilyn, Carly, and Ellie to claim sleeping rights next to G-Mama. One has to lose.

This particular night, Rilyn lost and had to sleep on the far side of the bed, next to the edge. I was in the middle of the bed with Carly on the right and Ellie resting on my left. Greer, as usual, was the first to slip into sweet slumber. Carly and Ellie followed closely and I managed to turn onto my side. Finally I heard Rilyn's soft breath, coming in regular, sleep-filled rhythm. Then, satisfied that all was well and everyone peacefully snoozing, I let the Sandman sprinkle his sleepy sand across my eyelids, and I fell under his spell, too.

Sometime during the deep night, I heard a whimpering, soft and frightened "G-Mama, G-Mama."

I quickly sprang upright and could barely see Rilyn standing beside the bed in darkness, wringing her hands and looking dazed. She had fallen off the bed and managed to stand: disoriented and afraid—not awake enough to climb back up onto the bed with us.

"G-Mama," she whispered, "I'm afraid and I don't know where I am."

I snapped on the small bedside light and quickly reached and held her close. "I'm here," I comforted. "Come on back to bed and you can sleep next to me."

She let me guide her into bed, her body trembling and her scared and bewildered face imprinted in my mind and would haunt me for days to come. She leaned into my arms, and I settled her to bed and covered her. My heart hurt to think that she had awoken and not realized where she was and she felt so alone, more than frightened, terror-filled there in the darkness. I snuggled close and held her next to me. I wanted her to know she was safe and loved, and that I was there to protect her.

We lay there, huddled together, and I waited and listened until her breathing became regular and she slept once more, comforted and safe.

≈

For God, who commanded the light to shine out of darkness, hath shined in our hearts to give the light of the knowledge of the Glory of God in the face of Jesus Christ.
2 Corinthians 4:6

≈

Imagine being in darkness and not knowing which way to go, whether the next step will be planted on solid ground or whether we will fall and tumble down through a cold, dark, and bottomless void. We cannot see anything—not even our hand in front of our face. We cannot feel anything on which to hold. Lost and we do not know where we are.

Such a terrifying thought.

Sadly, thousands upon thousands of people are standing in darkness, ignorant and helpless to find their way into the light. Some may be walking through the darkness and not realize there is a better way to live. As disciples, it is our mission to reach out and introduce these people to Jesus. A daunting and fearful challenge because we must put ourselves in scary, and many times evil, fearful situations. But it is our mission, and God is with us.

Thankfully, not all people have a heart so hardened that they are so lost they cannot be reached. There are people who have found their way through a dimly lit path and have reached a point close to the morning light, but are still teetering in the early softly-tinged edge. All they need to do is take one small step of faith to find themselves standing in soft, glowing, loving light. All we need to do is reach out a helping hand, offer support and guidance, and God will do the rest. Those lost in the edge of darkness will joyfully grasp our hand as they see the face of Jesus and step confidently into the light.

No longer lost in the dark and know where we are! Just as switching on a tiny nightlight, or lighting a candle in a dark room, we can disburse darkness and fear from our lives.

Darkness gobbles up every ray of light it can; sin gobbles up every spark of love and faith it can. God's loving light transforms the darkness—the very space surrounding us, into beauty and confidence.

When we are in the light and feel God's arms wrapped comfortingly around us, we know we are safe, just as Rilyn did. Standing on solid ground, being held close and comforted with loving arms! Such a wonderful, reassuring, safe feeling.

As we witness and gain strength through filling ourselves with God's grace, we can help those living in darkness find the light and learn to walk in it, confident that their steps will lead them along God's path. Still, they may stumble and hit rocky places, but we are there, too, to help and guide them. We can comfort and assure them that all is well, just as Rilyn was able to find peace and restful sleep again after her frightful ordeal. She was once again at peace, knowing she was safe and loved.

How the angels in Heaven will sing when the lost find their way, and we all shall revel in the light and in the Glory of God!

RILYN'S REVELATIONS

Good Summer Veggies

My lifelong friend, Elaine, and her husband, Dwain, keep me on track concerning the best varieties of vegetable seeds to plant. Early each spring, they begin pouring over seed catalogues and checking their cache of favorite seeds they have saved from the previous year's crop.

Dwain is diabetic and must have dialysis three times a week. All their trips to the doctor and early morning bouts for dialysis never seem to get them down. I sometimes think that anticipation for a good garden keeps their minds occupied and the excitement of planting is good therapy.

And, like them, Rilyn and I were yet again, during the early spring, preparing our soil for the vegetable garden and getting our seeds in order. Rambling through our seed packets, Rilyn spotted a pack of cucumber seeds. Not yet being able to read the long word printed across the face of the packet, she had to rely on the picture on the front to identify the veggie. Her mind jumped immediately to her reference of what type of seeds rattled around inside. She saw green cylinders that looked exactly like the sour whole dills chilling in a jar sitting in the refrigerator. "Oh, G-Mama," she exclaimed, "Let's plant these pickles!"

I suppose her innocence led her to be fooled. She only saw the outside appearance of the cucumber. She had never chosen to taste the raw veggie and relied on her prior knowledge of what cucumbers were—pickles. The cucumber she could pick from the pickle jar had been changed from its initial 'birth,' but she didn't know it.

I really had not planned to plant cucumbers. There were ample jars of last year's homemade pickles still on the shelf in the basement. Both mine and my husband's intestinal fortitudes no longer appreciate cucumbers in the raw, but Rilyn and I gathered up our seeds, fertilizer, gloves, and hoes and went out to plant us some pickles.

≈

Be not deceived, God is not mocked: for what soever a man soweth, that shall he also reap.
Galatians 6:7

≈

We planted Rilyn's seeds. When they grew and bloomed, she was thrilled. We talked about how, after bees wandered around inside the beautiful large, white bloom and visited another one, it carried pollen to help baby cucumbers form. I explained how they would grow fat and long on the vines. She did not realize, even then, that the newly growing cucumbers would not taste like her favorite sour pickles.

Summer days passed, the cucumbers matured and were finally ready to harvest. With her first bite, how disappointed Rilyn was—not the crunchy, sour, juicy pickle that bombarded her taste buds as she had expected. She had reaped what we had sown: plain ole' cucumbers.

One Sunday morning as I turned in my Bible to read along with the day's scripture message, I noticed where I had scribbled notes from a 1986 sermon. I attribute the notes to our then pastor, Gene Scott, who was always filled with such enthusiasm and love of sharing God's word that he infected us all. This goes right along with my thoughts on Rilyn's pickles, I thought. How God works to help me get His message out—even almost thirty years after the fact.

What we sow is what we get. But do we ever take the time to think about what we sow and what the consequences associated with our fruits may be? In today's hustle and bustle, scurrying around like those bees on Rilyn's cucumber blossoms, we say and do things that don't produce the results we meant for them to.

For example, as Gene said, instead of sowing seeds of success, we throw out seeds of failure—and we reap what we've inadvertently, or worse, deliberately, sown.

I read the short list of Gene's five points listed in the margin of my Bible. Thoughts wove through my head as I added my words to his ideas. First of five seeds to think about:

Sowing disobedience. When we disobey God's will and shut out His whispered plans for us, we will certainly reap destruction. We must submit our will, and accept His will, to avoid wretchedness and failure.

Sowing loose living. All might be well for a while. When we live 'loosely,' it seems that we have all the friends in the world. We have good times and lots of fun, and we do things, as we said in the 60s, because it feels good. In the end, all loose living brings us is loneliness. Eventually we will hit bottom and when we do, friends scatter, income is gone, and we are living in an awful void—without God (we think).

Sowing sin: simply, sin brings suffering. Suffering is like a blanket that covers not only us, the sinner, but also affects those around us who love us. Sin, the black, suffocating cloud that billows and tumbles, like that gray cloud that huddles over and creates misery for the cartoon character found in the Sunday comics, follows us and its wisps drift and twine outward to reach our family, neighbors, and friends making them sad, too. The good part is that if our loved ones are in a close relationship with God, they pray, and pray, and pray for us. With God's help, the suffering from sin will finally be blown away.

Sowing jealousy brings judgment. True, we should not judge others as we are not so perfect ourselves. When that ole' green dragon named Jealousy comes to live as our house pet, we begin to look and see things that others have that we would love to have for our own: we become envious of things that others have and we want them for ourselves. Jealousy is not simply a want or wish, it is a deep desire that causes us to say and do things that are hateful and hurtful. Through our actions, others make a sometimes hard decision—they find ways to stay away from us. We lose our friends, our happiness shared in our get-togethers, and all we can do is stay at home and keep our house pet, Jealousy, fed and taken care of.

Who really wants a pet like that?

And last: hardness a hardness of our hearts, our minds, and our thoughts. This brings heartache that can only be healed through the goodness and grace of God. How my heart aches for those with the heartache that comes from hardness!

Rilyn, in the end, even though she was very disappointed of the zero crop of pickles, was thrilled with her abundant crop of cucumbers. She reveled in picking them and putting them in her garden basket. We carried them inside and washed and bagged a few, and she shared her fruits with her grandparents and great-grandparents.

But I just bet she won't be fooled again! She'll make sure whatever she sows will be just what she plans to harvest.

RILYN'S REVELATIONS

More Than a Flower Pot Filler

I recall the statement I heard from a fruit and vegetable vendor when I was shopping at her wagon one warm, late summer afternoon 'up north'. I asked if she had any fresh okra for sale. That brought on a gutsy belly laugh pouring from deep inside, sounding much like the bray of a hungry donkey. She wheezed as she wiped happy-tears, "Honey, the only reason we grow okra up here is to dry the pods and use them as fillers in dried flower arrangements."

So much for having fresh, fried okra for supper that evening.

Here in the south I have eaten fried and boiled okra all my life. I fondly think of Grandmother Gore's words at dinner (lunch, for those who aren't southern country) after she had placed some tender pods of okra on top of the fresh peas to tenderize as the peas boiled. After the blessing and my dad had helped himself to the cornbread and peas, he placed several slippery, tender okra pods on his plate. We filled our plates too, minus the boiled okra for me, and grandmother looked at our plates as we sat around the table. Her next words were one of the few times she quipped a joke. "You'd better cross your legs while you eat that!" she said through a mile-wide grin and nodded at the okra piled high on daddy's plate.

At first, young as I was at the time, I just didn't get it. Later, when I tried to eat the boiled version, I came to fully understand exactly what Grandmother meant. That stuff had the capabilities of slipping and sliding right on through a body—in one end and quickly out the other!

Okra is always one of our yearly plantings in our garden. Daddy helped start Granddaddy and me with our first garden, giving us enough of his precious okra seeds to plant from his saved cache from his previous garden's crop. With these, we could plant a couple of rows. After that, it was up to us to gather a few dried pods in the fall and preserve our seed supply for the next year's planting.

So this past spring we planted the seeds; okra plants sprouted in thick, grew quickly and I thinned them (wincing with each extraction! How I hated to waste good plants). As painful as it was for me, it had to be done for maximum pod bearing during summer. Finally, after weeks of watching and waiting, long green pods were at last standing at attention on the stalks, ready to cut. Time to harvest.

Rilyn carried her basket to the garden and kept my ears buzzing as we walked the rows and I cut and tossed the tender green pods into it.

Back inside the house, she helped me wash our okra. Then she took a break and went to play while I cut the pods and prepared it to fry. She returned to check on my progress and found the bowl full of okra cut into small, uniform green wheels, but I had not yet battered it. Always ready to help, she scooted her stool to the sink and washed her hands. "Can I help?" she asked.

"Sure," I replied. "You can get out the flour and cornmeal so we can batter the okra."

As she moved across the kitchen to get the flour, she spied the okra piled high, like a mini-volcano, in the bowl. She deftly reached over to level the okra even with the edge of the bowl and got a first-hand feel of fresh-cut okra.

"Eewww," she said, quickly jerking her hand away and giving the slippery okra 'juice' hanging and dangling from her fingers a shake. It required more than one shake to dislodge the goo. "This stuff is snotty!" she moaned.

I laughed as I handed her a paper towel to wipe her hand. "It is now, but you know how you love to pop it like popcorn into your mouth after it's fried."

"Yeah," she murmured. "You can finish this. I'll just wait 'til it's done."

≈

> . . . for the Lord seeth; for a man looketh on the outward appearance, but the Lord looketh on the heart.
> 1 Samuel 16:7

≈

How often have we formed an opinion from first impressions? Admittedly, sometimes the first impressions stick, but more likely than not when I have formed my ideas before I get to know the person, my impression changes as I get more familiar with them.

During my teens, after I learned to drive and obtained my driver's license, I drove my Papa and Grandmother Gore (Papa was the minister) to church and to visit sick and shut-in church members. One summer while I was there for my weekly stay, I met a very pretty, lively girl during week long revival. She chatted and laughed, and most of the boys gathered around her before and after the meetings like kids to candy. I told myself she was a flirt, and I did not make any effort to be friendly to her when she tried to start a conversation with me. Truthfully, I was jealous, but refused to admit it.

The week ended, but I never responded to her offers of friendship, nor did I make any effort to befriend her.

A few weeks after revival my grandparents visited us. Grandmother Gore asked me if I remembered Gloria. I nodded that I did.

"You know her dad left her and her mom when she was a little girl and her mom became an alcoholic," she added.

I was shocked. I had not known.

"She came to school drunk one day last week and was expelled. When her mother got home from work, she found Gloria lying unconscious on her bedroom floor, but was able to get help in time to get her to the hospital. She'd tried to commit suicide."

I had to leave the room. I was shocked and speechless. My heart raced and my body felt numb. I wanted to implode to the point of disappearing. I had been so uncaring and so mean. My impression had been so wrong.

Another time, much later, during my teaching career, a parent requested a parent conference. We set a meeting time, and I sat at the conference table as the child's father entered the room. I know my eyes almost popped out of my head and he could hear the bones in my neck snapping as I quickly turned my head away from his deep brown eyes and bored my own onto my grade book lying open on my lap. The man had prison tattoos down each arm. He had a Foo-Man-Chu type mustache and he and was big and he was burly-looking. A no-nonsense type of guy. Not at all what I had expected. I knew he could feel my intimidation and see my nervousness as he sat in the chair across the table from me.

But after only a few words, I realized he was so agreeable! Our meeting was not at all what I had imagined, at first glance, our conversation would be. When I first laid eyes on him, I imagined he would be telling me how to teach and what he would do if I didn't get the job done. I had only paid attention to his outward appearance and had made a quick judgment based solely on that: my preconceived notion. I quickly learned what he was like inside . . .

We talked and his concern for his son came shining through. His desire to find out what he and his wife could do to help his son and to support me and my efforts was obvious. Sitting there, I no longer saw the tats or thought his eyes were hard or threatening; I saw, as well as felt, the love and concern he had for his son.

Later, he and his wife, his son (my student), along with their younger son, visited our church. They became regulars and now are an important part of our church family.

How I had missed the mark and formed totally wrong impressions of both Gloria and this father. What I had initially seen was no way what reality was. Gloria was depressed and sad. She flirted and made herself the center of attention to cover and bolster her true feelings of inadequacy and loneliness. My student's father was kind and concerned, not at all a bad, tough guy.

Looking beyond the outward visible attributes and seeing what is inside is essential for not letting first impressions prevent us from finding new friends, seeing new things, and learning new lessons. People or situations may seem fearful or uncaring at first glance, but taking time to uncover, reveal, and discover their true identity, all they have inside to give, present us with surprise blessings. If we just take time to look for the beauty inside.

But we must also beware of evil that hides behind beauty, like the wolf that slips into sheep's skin to fool even the shepherd. Beware of the outside; take time to check out the inside.

The devil's devious mind is clever and crafty. He knows our carnal passions and he seeks to satisfy our desires by leading and introducing us to circumstances that deceive us so that we misinterpret that beauty. We see beauty, and it becomes desirous to us and, all the while, there is really ugly, underlying sin. We think our physical desires, wishes and longings are going to be easily met. We are impressed by his temptations and sometimes jump right in—not looking beneath the obvious, only to find despair and rot that Satan uses to hurt our relationship with God, family, and friends. Satan wishes to destroy our Godly influence and kill our influence as

God's witness. We must continuously be watchful and take time to get to know the real deal.

After hearing Grandmother Gore's words about Gloria's failed suicide attempt, the next time I visited my grandparents and we attended church, when Gloria invited me over to spend the afternoon with her, I went. And I had loads of fun with my new found friend.

When my student's family visited our church, I was in line to welcome them. They have stayed and became loved members of our congregation. They add so much to out worship and always help with our fellowship activities. We are blessed to have them.

That okra was slimy and gooey. If Rilyn had seen it before her first taste, more than likely she would never have taken that first bite. When the bowl of fresh okra was battered and fried up all crispy and crunchy and hot, it was delicious.

First impressions can often throw us off base, and we miss some wonderful blessings. What blessings Rilyn and I would have missed if we had stuck with our first impressions— me with people and her with okra. What, at first glance, looked like something we would not like or be comfortable with, actually turned out to be quite nice! We can experience people and things in wonderful new ways to enrich our lives, and not limit them to being simply 'dried up flower pot fillers'.

Take that extra moment, have two grains of patience, a huge scoop of kindness, and keep our hearts and minds open. Get past, as Rilyn described, the 'snottiness,' and find true beauty that God has hidden in special places and in people that will surprise and be blessings to us all.

RILYN'S REVELATIONS

OUTSIDE

Inside

By Ellie

Smooching, Smooching

Our log house has been built in stages covering almost thirty years: first we constructed the basic saltbox style home; added the wide front porch later, and then we erected a pole garage which was enclosed years after. Next, our back screened-in porch, then an east side covered porch and deck, followed much later with a west porch, and finally back deck with steep steps leading down to the hot tub sitting on its own covered deck. During this time of transition, the screen wire enclosing the back porch has been replaced with windows, making a nice warm spot to read or play. We didn't know until later just how in style we were.

While Ginger was attending Auburn University in Alabama, one of her friends often referred to her parent's Florida Room. Not familiar with the term, Ginger asked what she meant by her words.

"Oh, a south-facing room with three sides glassed in where mom and dad can sit in the sunshine and relax," her friend explained.

"I see," Ginger replied with a thoughtful nod. "We call ours the back porch!"

Our Florida Room is the home of Phoebe, our Cockatiel, the place where Granddaddy 'plays' on his computer, where the extra dining table and chairs are, and where the two toy boxes and child's table and chairs are. It's a great place to play, and we all love spending time on the back porch.

The girls especially love to play out there. Sometimes they line up all the chairs, large and small, train-style or schoolroom style, and fill them with bears, monkeys, penguins, and other stuffed friends and have a ball. Hours of arranging and rearranging, deep discussions, and imaginary events transpire during their playtime spent in the special room.

The kiddie table doubles as their art table. Paper, colored pencils, markers, and scissors are often scattered on the table and in the floor and chair seats. Ellie, our three-year-old, loves to mark and color as much as anyone. One afternoon as Rilyn and Carly were busy practicing writing their letters at the table, Ellie was busy, too, doing some writing herself.

I could hear their play as I worked nearby in the kitchen. As usual, Rilyn was the teacher and Carly was her pupil. I assumed Ellie was, too, but didn't hear her voice as part of the trio. All of a sudden, I hear Rilyn's voice breaking the peacefulness like a fire alarm screaming full force, as I rushed over to look into the play-porch I noticed both Carly's and Rilyn's attention focused on Ellie, who was in the corner of the room near Granddaddy's computer desk, out of my view. I could tell something drastic had happened by the 'uh-oh' look on both the older girls' faces.

After a quiet moment, Rilyn spoke. "Ellie," she said, "you shouldn't have written all over Granddaddy's chair with that marker. He's gonna have a kissy fit!"

I walked in. Sure enough, there stood Ellie, guilty as charged, standing beside the computer chair with marker in hand. The chair had been decorated beautifully with Ellie's specialty: hundreds of small curly scripts dotted the back and seat of the blue chair. And not only the chair, but both her arms, as well.

Well, no need to fuss. What was done was done. "Come on, Ellie," I said. "Let's get you cleaned up before Granddaddy sees this and has one of his kissy fits!"

Needless to say, that ended the art lessons on the back porch for a while.

≈

Doth a fountain send forth at the same place sweet water and bitter? . . . Can the fig tree, my brethren, bear olive berries? Either a vine, figs? So can no fountain yield both salt water and fresh?
James 3:12

≈

Our lips move and words tumble out like creek water over high rocks. Words, as they are uttered from our lips, flow as a fountain. How they can be used as a sweet wash to heal, comfort, and express love and care—or be bitter, mean, and hateful. Words: invisible, unbreakable, untouchable. Words can be soft as butterfly kisses or hard and sharp as a sword. Words are powerful enough to calm the angry and anxious, or to stifle creativity and self-confidence, mighty enough to cower the bully, or wrap the lost in love.

Words used while having a 'hissy fit' can be strong enough to kill a soul, or uttered in 'kissy fit' mode can uplift the masses. Words rushing from our lips, how they can be used— to hurt, break hearts, discourage success, and create insecurities, or used to love and uplift, heal and make safe.

I thought of Rilyn's expression and how a kissy fit is quite an oxymoron: kisses are expressions of love and sweetness; fits express anger, disappointment, and loss of control. What are our everyday words expressing?

How we choose words and let them fly past our lips affect others. Which kind of words should we choose to use—kissy fit or hissy fit?

Words we use to describe others and ourselves reflect our true feelings about others and how we feel about ourselves. What do we create with words? Are we prone to kissy fits, or to pitch hissy fits? Do we destroy or twist the truth or do we uplift the truth and spread grace, love, healing, and peace?

We should be watchful and thoughtful of how we choose words that pass our lips. I have seen children broken, shy, and so low in self-confidence simply because they have heard over and over how inadequate or stupid they are.

On the other hand, Karee, my niece who taught special needs as an inclusion teacher, was surprised at how well her students were functioning in the regular classroom. One day as she sat with one of her students during lunch, one little girl said, "Mrs. Payne, I'm so glad you come in our room to help teach us gifted kids."

Karee, surprised at the misconception, expressed her enjoyment at coming to the classroom. She didn't correct the student's perception, but instead confirmed how proud she was of how well the girl was doing.

Someone must have told the little girl that Karee was one of the gifted teachers. The child made a logical assumption: this gifted teacher came into her classroom to teach her, therefore, she must be very smart. She began improving, more confident, and proud of her accomplishments.

Karee, like many educators, realizes the full potential of guiding children to be positive and believe in their success and strengths. She taught them with patience and love. She let her words uplift and build confidence in her students who were, in reality, below regular grade level abilities. She used words to love and uplift.

Yep, it works! The words children hear that define their personality and abilities are those they exhibit when they become adults.

We need more kissy fits. We must always make the effort to say things that will make people feel worthwhile, and not what they are not. As Pastor Jared Evans would say, we need to use words to encourage, guide, teach, express love, care, and share God's love. Some examples are:

- ♥ I love you. (I cannot stand you.)
- ♥ You are beautiful and smart. (You are an ugly idiot.)
- ♥ I need you. (Get away from me.)
- ♥ You are precious to me. (You are worthless.)

Let your lips form God's words, and let the truth of the words shine through your eyes. Children recognize fakes and untruthful words. Fake eyes and fake smiles—fake words. Our words must be genuine and our love show through our deeds and demeanors that will reach out and warm their hearts.

It was useless to try to remove Ellie's permanent pen artwork from the chair. No need for Granddaddy to have a hissy fit. All we could do was laugh about it, pucker up, and have a good ole' kissy fit!

Cheryl Gore Pollard

When Ya Gotta' Go, Ya Gotta' Go

One afternoon the Magnificent Seven, Granddaddy, and I were outside enjoying one of the first really nice spring days. Granddaddy and I watched as the Grands played on the swing set or dug in the sandpile. Hayden was overseeing Isabelle, pushing her in her baby swing and laughing right along with her; Ellie had settled belly down on one swing and was curling it around, making the ropes twine tightly and squealing with delight after she lifted her feet and her body flew around fast as a whirly gig in full wind. Greyson busily tossed his baseball high and deftly caught it as it came plummeting back to his glove, and Greer, Carly, and Rilyn were busy building 'frog houses' and fairy castles in the sand. Granddaddy and I were basking in the beauty of the day, enjoying our Grands having such a good time.

We watched as Greer supervised the construction of a sand castle her younger cousins were building—stacking ramparts, towers, and digging a special moat. Carly and Rilyn stayed busy racing to and fro from the daisies to daylilies and on to the Lantanas that bloomed profusely in the yard, plucking the colorful flowers and petals and bustling back to present them to Greer. She and her two helpers carefully chose the perfect spot to place each bloom on the castle, just where the fairies would enjoy the royal decorations as they came to sleep in their new home that evening.

I watched as the Magnificent Seven laughed and played and made wonderful memories together on this beautiful spring afternoon. Suddenly, Rilyn jumped up and ran into the house like a rabbit being chased by a hound. A few short minutes later, she ran back out hollering, "G-Mama, G-Mama!"

"What now?" I thought.

She skidded to a stop beside my lawn chair and planted her feet firmly apart, stuck her fists atop her hips and exclaimed, "I fell in the toilet!"

The look on my face must have said it all, because before I could sputter a word, she continued, "I was in a real big hurry and didn't look when I sat down and someone had left the girl seat up and I sat on the boy seat and my bottom fell in!" She was most indignant.

"Did you get dried off and finish up your business?" I asked nonchalantly.

She nodded yes, but the deep frown exhibiting her disdain remained across her forehead.

"So you're fine then; go along and play," I instructed, and waved her off.

As Rilyn stalked away to the sandpile, I glanced at Greyson standing close by, pitching his ball low, in mild concentration. He'd had one ear cocked toward our conversation, listening all the while like a sly fox honing in on an unsuspecting hen as Rilyn described sitting on the toilet's 'boy seat'. Our eyes met, and for an instant I saw bright, tell-tale glints dancing in his deep brown eyes. As he looked away, I watched as a discreet, knowing grin inched its way across his face. He skipped expertly along the grass and tossed his ball the highest ever. And caught it without missing a beat.

RILYN'S REVELATIONS

≈

*For God hath not called us unto uncleanness,
but unto holiness.
1 Thessalonians 4:7*

≈

How many times have we asked, "How in the world did I get in this mess?" Or found ourselves in a situation where the only thought that came to mind was the old saying 'look before you leap'?

For me, most often than not, these thoughts come to me while I am dealing with some aspect of the Lord's work. How easily to be so zealous about beginning a new church project, tackling a mission with a friend, or making a promise to a child or friend, and finding myself sitting on the edge of the 'boy seat' of the toilet, balancing precariously to keep from falling in the dirty water—simply because I'd not paid careful attention to what I had been doing. Often I found that I had not prepared myself properly for the task or made the best plans to organize my project. Not really thinking and planning in a Godly manner caused me to 'fall in the toilet'.

God has everything prepared for us—He ordained it from the very first moment of creation in His perfect will. In this, His will is for us to walk in perfect, complete fellowship with Him. He has implicit plans for us from the moment we enter the world at birth; a wonderful plan that Jesus set in motion at His birth and culminated as He suffered on the cross. After He was placed in His sepulchre and three days later that massive stone rolled away from that grave, a wonderful plan was sealed and put in motion for us by our Savior. If we could only follow that perfect path that God has set for us and not get in too big a hurry, keep our minds on God's plan, and be SO aware of what we do and how to do it, we could maintain our clean, Godly lives, living and breathing in His perfect will.

But we are human and have been given the gift of choice. Sometimes we forget to be careful of the choices we make and how we choose, and we fall in the toilet. God permits this and provides for our safekeeping through what we might call His permissive will. We see our faults and failures, come to Him in repentance, and He forgives us—never having stopped loving us.

When we do find ourselves in a precarious position and we must face our sins and repent, we must do as Rilyn did—hop out the second we realize we are in a bad, dirty place, clean ourselves off, get the job done, fix the problem (with Godly wisdom) and confess our mistake so we will be sure not to get ourselves in that situation again.

God also has an ultimate will in store for those of us who persevere, striving to live our lives for Him. We will be met by St. Peter at the Pearly Gates with welcoming, open arms. In His will, this ultimate will, we find ourselves in that beautiful, everlasting place, holy and perfectly at home with Him.

Being aware and double checking to make sure everything is right makes everything move smoother. Remembering to check and put the girl's seat down if we need to, and to replace it where it usually rests if we have raised it, will certainly make completing any job a snap!

Sitting in the spring air, watching our Grands playing happily and peacefully together made a lovely day. Especially for me--and I know those fairies loved their fancy castle for the night!

RILYN'S REVELATIONS

Hip Hop

Greer, our eleven-year-old and twin sister to Greyson, recently began dance lessons. Hip Hop. The moves were hard for her to master, especially since her and her mom's schedule only opted for her to enroll in the second session dance class. She had to work extra hard to catch up since she'd never had the first dancing session. She loves it, and looks forward to practice and the social interaction with the other dancers.

One afternoon, when I arrived to pick up the Grands for our weekly Friday night at G-Mamma's and Granddaddy's, she was especially excited. She had just gotten her new hip hop outfit to wear in the recital and could hardly wait to show it to me. It was cute and colorful, and I could tell by her wide grin and twinkling eyes she was proud of it.

The following Wednesday after our busy weekend, Ginger sent a picture via phone of what Greer had come up with to wear to dance as a practice outfit. She had taken one of her tee shirts and cut the sleeves off and split it down the sides, making a dandy, but revealing, hip hop practice shirt. Naturally, Rilyn was in the room watching all the shirt modifications as Greer designed and created her practice outfit, and was right there that afternoon when Greer modeled it for her mom.

"I think you need something underneath," Ginger remarked. "It's a little open down the sides. I can see some skin, and I know your dad won't go for it."

It was cut much down the sides, leaving little to the imagination. She looked like she was more ready for the beach instead of the dance floor—maybe snipping just a little too much. The same as her friend's, but a little different at the same time.

"Paige has a shirt like this and it's okay with her dad," Greer said. "She wears hers to practice. I don't know why I can't."

That was it for Rilyn. Before Ginger had a chance to reply, Rilyn's comment put an end to Greer's argument. "Well, Greer," Rilyn said, as she cocked her hip to one side and flipped her blonde curls back across her shoulder with her hand. And, in her matter of fact tone lectured, "You're not Paige and Chuck isn't her dad."

No use trying to argue with that.

Ginger turned away to hide her grin. Greer huffed and puffed upstairs to change.

≈

*..., hear the instructions of thy father,
and forsake not the law of thy mother.
Proverbs 1:8*

≈

When it comes to teaching children, their parents, or primary caretakers, are the ones who shape and mold young minds and bodies into thoughtful, well-thought-of adults. Rules and limits are essential for children to follow in order to become productive, successful grownups. There is always the tug-of-war between what the children want to do and what the family rule says she, or he, can or cannot do. Adult guidance and protective leadership are the glue that keeps any child's feet anchored to the ground and helps them make good, solid decisions.

Greer was simply following the style of dress that some of her friends liked—maybe hers was a little extreme but, more importantly, she wanted to do her thing and fit in. Thankfully, she has a father and mother who are involved in her activities and are accountable of their role in her growing up. She may have been disappointed that her outfit did not meet her dad's standards, but she understood. I am proud of her for that.

I am grateful that my children have set guidelines for their own children and explain to them why the rules and instructions are important. My grandchildren have the wonderful opportunity to observe their parents as they make decisions based on good choices, watch and listen as their parents pray, and know that their parents would do whatever necessary to keep them safe and out of harm's way.

As a child, I always knew my father was there if I needed him. He never judged nor belittled me, but I was fully aware the times I disappointed him or let him down. Our Heavenly Father has given us rules and guidelines in stories and teachings of Jesus. He, like my dad, feels disappointment when we do not follow His instructions. He, like my dad, is always ready to listen to our supplications and forgive us. How blessed we are!

I am saddened when I see children who are, for whatever reason, growing up without one or both parents. Their lives are truly lived harder than their peers who have the love and security of both parents. I have been a single mother, and I know how everyday pressures tended to wear me down. Work, finances, and time seemed to jumble all together, and how hard I tried to provide for all my children's needs. I provided as I could with limited income. The child support barely covered the car payment and my once-a-month salary was stretched really thin. There was always so much to do. In spite of my best intentions, I often fell short. There were huge gaps where I didn't recognize and attend to my children's needs as I should have. Mistakes? Yeah! Things I wish I could go back and redo? Yeah! But I knew God would take care of us. And he did. He sent friends and neighbors, family and church family, and somehow, someway, our needs were always met. I am blessed that I have two wonderful families who survived these lean years: my daughter, Ginger, and Chuck's and my son, Sonny, and Phyllis's, who have grown strong and flourished. Good things CAN come from bad experiences.

I am saddened, too, when I see children who have parents who are burdened with low income, no housing, or lack of a way to provide for their children. They try so hard to provide for their family, and often it is little more than their faith and the grace of God that holds them together.

Sadder still are the children whose parents are incarcerated, addicted, or 'gone'. We as Christians must reach out and be the nurturer and role model, and help provide support and confidence they need.

As Rilyn told Greer, she's who she is and her daddy is the one she must obey, trust, and depend upon. Just as God is ours. God sees us as His children, and we must look to Him and trust in Him to guide and direct us in our growth and decisions. That's the rule we can follow to dance our way to a happier life.

Goin' Through the Motions

Chuck is a busy dad. If time be totaled, there are almost as many days he is away from the house on business as there are nights as he is home. When he is home, Rilyn takes full advantage of being close to him and involved in everything he's doing.

One night after dinner had been cleared away and homework finished, the family gathered in the den to watch TV. Rilyn piled herself in Chuck's lap, informing him of what had been going on at school and at home during his recent absence. Chatter, chatter, chatter, like a blue jay sitting on top of a fencepost telling the news to his neighbors.

"Rilyn, please be quiet," Hayden, the oldest asked. "I want to hear the TV."

Rilyn rolled her eyes and continued her conversation with Chuck. He inserted an occasional 'Okay' or nodded in agreement to her ongoing dialogue. It did not take long for Rilyn to realize his interest was first on the TV and second on her story.

She sat back and said, "Daddy, daddy," and when she saw he had turned his face to her, she was assured that she finally had his full attention.

"What?" he asked.

"Do you think I talk too much?"

"Well, sometimes you do talk a lot," he replied.

"Huh," Rilyn puffed, then, thinking hard, she clasped her hands together underneath her chin and propped it on her fist. Suddenly she sat straight and said, "I guess I do talk a lot—but it gives my mouth something to do."

Chuck just gave up.

≈

(5) And when thou prayest, thou shalt not be like the hypocrites are: for they love to pray standing in the synagogues and in the corners of the streets, that they may be seen of men. Verily I say unto you, They have their reward.

(7) But when ye pray, use not vain repetitions, as the heathens do: for they think that they shall be heard for their much speaking. Be not ye therefore like unto them; for your Father knoweth what things ye have need of,

before ye ask him.

Matthew 6:5 and 7

≈

Do we consider our sincerity when we pray? How do we pray? Do we pray out of habit, unthinking and without heartfelt concern? Are we as the hypocrites and heathens and pray because our mouths need something to do?

God forbid! We all probably know, or remember from our childhood, that person who was invariably called upon to pray during those hot summer revival nights with only church windows opened for an occasional cool breeze to drift in. The one person who could pray—and pray—and pray, and we hardly knew afterward what was said. I recall listening to these 'odes' (as I refer to the prayer) being offered up, that while standing in prayer, I had to hold onto the bench in front of me to keep from dozing off! I certainly wasn't encouraged to pray if that was my model to follow.

How do we pray? Are we selfish prayers? Do we give genuine thanks for our blessings? Do we ask for his blessings for our neighbors, friends, government, military, and medical and police forces? How about the sick and those mourning the loss of a loved one? Are our comforting words to others coming from our heart, or do we speak the words that we're supposed to?

God wants us to come to Him with expectations to be blessed. Sure, He knows what we need, and what we want, too, but we need to acknowledge, ask Him, supplicate Him for our needs. He is there especially for us to talk to, and He is always ready to listen.

"I can't pray because I don't know what to say," I often hear. I really don't think God cares how big our vocabulary is or how great our grammar is—He simply wants us to talk to Him.

"I don't know how to pray," is another excuse I hear. I think of being in a restaurant and ordering a salad. I like salads, and thankfully, I usually have a variety from which to choose. Whether I choose Taco, House, Chicken, Garden, Caesar, or some other, I have my salad. Each may be composed of different ingredients and all will have a little different flavor, but each is a salad.

When my order comes, I have my salad. Others sitting at the table watch as theirs arrive too, and are different, but it doesn't matter. They all look good and taste good, and they all 'hit the spot,' as Granddaddy says.

Prayer is like that. God doesn't care which words we use or how our prayer is put together or variations of thought we use. In the end, whatever we say thoughtfully from our hearts is precisely what we need to communicate with Him, and He understands. He's happy to get our 'salad' that we've made just for Him.

And in case we're still in doubt, Jesus taught us a simple model anyone can use. The words He taught His disciples over two-thousand years ago are still just as fresh as they were then. He told us to pray by:

<u>Addressing Him personally</u>: *Our Father, who art in Heaven.* We acknowledge that He is our FATHER! A father for all of us! Halleluiah and wonder!

<u>Honoring Him</u>: *Hallowed be Thy name.* He is the Holy One.

<u>Asking for joy and peace</u>: *Thy Kingdom come; Thy will be done on Earth as it is in Heaven.* I can't imagine the joy and wonder that I will experience in Heaven—much less envisioning His kingdom coming!

<u>Asking for provisions as we need them</u>: *Give us this day our daily bread.* He provides for our needs, just as He gave manna, quail, and water to Moses and the wandering Hebrew people as they needed it.

<u>Asking for forgiveness</u>: *and forgive us of our sins as we forgive others.* Such an important lesson—we are forgiven *as we forgive others*—can we love enough to forgive those who have hurt us? We must have faith and forgiveness, for without that personal forgiveness, God will not forgive us.

<u>Asking for protection</u>: *Lead us not into temptation, but deliver us from evil.* Such power and assurance: to know we walk wrapped in the saving arms of God. Even as we sometimes walk in the Shadow of Death. He is our protector.

<u>Giving Him our praise</u>: *for Thine is the Kingdom, and Power, and Glory forever . . .* wow! He has it all.

Amen

How simple is that?

Prayer and comforting words should be thoughtful and personal, not some rambling account or a long speech intended to impress others. It shouldn't be said because our mouths need something to do—it should be spoken in our own way to God, and after is the time when we should be quiet, listen, and expect His response.

Thank You for Our Blessings

Can't Those Girls Leave My Nativity Alone?

Christmas is a wonderful time around the Pollard House. I usually wait until the Grands are here so they can help me decorate for the holidays. We have stuff hung, set, strung, and arranged in every nook and cranny possible.

Greer claims the Snow Babies, and busies herself arranging her little bundled up porcelain babies with their snowmen or sleds, skating on the glass pond, or playing in the snow. Then she carefully sprinkles the plastic snow over her setting to complete her display.

Hayden and Greyson are becoming less and less involved—I guess getting excited over some glass and plastic ornaments and a tree is not a guy thing, but I do manage to persuade them to help get the tree in from the garage and set it up in the Florida Room. As boxes appear from the closet in the basement, the boys do like to dig in the ornament tubs to find ones they remember and have a special memory attached to or to seek out new ornaments that I've sneaked in during the year. They soon tire and retire to the den to hang out and play with almost a year-old Isabelle, keeping her from getting underfoot in our back porch until we are ready for the final decorations.

The Four Musketeers – Greer, Rilyn, Carly, and Ellie – are my tried and true helpmates. Oh, how they love to pull out, ooh, and aww over the ornaments and decorations. Greer gently removes the delicate tree trimmings from their year-long rest and passes them to her three helpers. They always get ahead of me, and I'm amused when we're almost out of ornaments and I notice the top third of the tree has none at all—it's still bare and green. That's when I call in Greer's special help. She moves from the now empty tubs and stands beside the tree, carefully looking and deciding where to move ornaments from below to the top to complete the tree. I notice this Christmas how she's grown tall and slender, like the proverbial bean pole. She readily chooses ornaments that the younger girls have placed, as high as they were able to, and moved them. She reaches high to rehang the pretty baubles around the top.

Then eleven-month-old Isabelle walks in to join the fun. Somehow Hayden and Greyson have kept her occupied and out of our hair, but she's worn them down. She's escaped and has come to check us out. Now all the girls are kept busy replacing ornaments that Isabelle chooses and quickly grabs off the tree! She's amazed at her first view of a Christmas tree.

One tradition all the Grands must be present for is placing the angel, crocheted from thin, white yarn by talented Aunt Denise, on top of the tree. When the boys hear my call, they come running. They stand around the tree and I plug in the extension. Lights glow and reflect off the glass balls. Just for a magic instant, everyone stands quietly, soaking in the beauty of our Christmas tree. There in the Christmas silence, I can almost hear the flashing glints bouncing off the colorful glass balls as the added late afternoon incoming sunlight beams through the windows. Sparkles twinkle and jump from one to the other as the decorations dip and dance on the branches. God provides His light too, and what a sight!

Then the solitude is broken as an argument breaks out about whose turn it is to place the angel on the topmost bough. Voices, like a flock of cackling pond geese, echo across the sunporch until it is decided whose turn it is to do the honors. I hand the angel to Hayden, the honoree for this year's placement, and we stand back quietly and watch as he, even as tall as he is, reaches high, stretching to his tiptoes, to balance the heirloom angel on the very top stem. Then we stand back and admire, eyes shining in Christmas appreciation. I hear as the children utter a sweet sigh, and then they wander back to their usual pastime activities. But another memory has been born, one to keep and cherish for years and years.

Another Christmas tradition is setting up the Nativities. I love Nativities and I think I have passed that love along to all the grandchildren. Last count, I had fifteen, and I have added a couple of new ones this year. The girls always have loved playing with them, and I love watching them enjoy the sets. A couple of years ago, I noticed a particularly large-piece Nativity at a thrift store. It wasn't really pretty, and it was probably made during the 70s when painting ceramics was really the hot thing for bored housewives to do. (I was one of them!) This one didn't have much detail or colorful painting involved; it was blah brown. *Hmmm*, I thought. This is perfect for the Grands to play with, it was certainly large enough for them to pick up and hold easily, it had lots and lots of pieces, and if a piece was accidently broken, no big deal.

I snatched it up for a great price and added it to my collection.

I usually display that Nativity on an antique washstand beside the front door. One afternoon, my friend, Becky, visited. As she was leaving, she noticed it and oohed, "You have a chocolate Nativity!" she exclaimed.

I gleamed as her bright idea made the lightbulb in my head flash. That's what I had all right, a chocolate Nativity! It wasn't blah at all!

There's a hodgepodge of characters that make up the display. The person who chose the personalities to put this Nativity together probably loves Nativities as much as I do, because it's big and it has plenty of characters. Naturally there are Mary, Joseph, and Baby Jesus, the Wise Men, and the Angel. The artist added a couple of shepherds, three sheep, a cow, a donkey, two camels, and a couple of odds: a goat and some guy kneeling holding a tray of fruit. It works, though.

This Christmas I put it out and placed my individuals just so, as I always do: the Wise Men on the right, coming from the east with the camels; the shepherd and his sheep on the left, (I let the goat be in the group, too); the fruit guy near the Wise Men; the cow and donkey behind the Blessed Family, and the angel balanced behind the whole group. Then I went my merry way.

Imagine my surprise when a few minutes later I passed by and there were my people and animals all mixed up, squished in a bunch on the middle top of the washstand.

I moved the characters back to their chosen places.

Next trip by the Nativity site, the same thing: everybody all bunched up in a wad.

I placed them once more in their proper positions.

The third time I found the Nativity all smushed together, my surprise turned into irritation. I rearranged my Nativity back onto its appropriate display site and slipped around the kitchen/foyer area to keep an inconspicuous eye on my grouping and catch the conspirators. I went about my pots and pans motions to give the impression that I was really busy in the kitchen. I was most convincing.

It didn't take long for me to see what had been going on. I realized Rilyn and Carly had wanted an ice cream or icy-pop and exited through the front door to go to the garage to help themselves to their treats in the freezer where the frozen delights are kept. When they reached the door, they'd spied the Nativity and paused long enough to move everything as they liked it. Same thing when they came by again—to get Ellie a treat.

This time, as I watched and listened, I learned Carly and Rilyn planned to go out to ride bicycles, and before they reached for the doorknob, they again paused by the Nativity and huddled around the Bethlehem family. I silently watched, intrigued, as they whispered to each other with their heads huddled close. The bright blonde head leaned toward the shining red head and they talked quietly as they deftly moved characters around. I couldn't hear what they were saying, but knew they were in deep discussion and making sure their decisions for placing the people and animals fit just so. Their little heads bobbed up and down in agreement, and their small hands moved with care and precision. Finally satisfied, Carly grabbed the doorknob, opened the door and they skipped outside.

I moved to the washstand and looked, carefully this time. The people were not haphazardly wadded together; they were arranged in a circle; the animals filling in the spaces between. And right in the center was the Christ Child, lying quietly in His manger.

. . . And the greatest gift of all, love? Not quite. It was more: the gift of a child, the Christ Child.

Tears came into my eyes and I had to swallow hard to get the lump that had formed there out of my throat. It was as if a halo appeared around my Nativity and in that instant, I was hit with this final revelation: Wasn't this exactly where we should be in our everyday existence? We should be keeping Christ as the center and holding fast with our fellow Christians to form an unending circle of love and faith, keeping His love and grace intact. All creation, the earth and all that's in it. worshiping and praising Jesus and preserving Him in the center of our lives.

We are blessed with the births of children whether they are our own, our grandchildren, nieces or nephews, or adopted. Children: our Blessed Gifts.

I wiped my nose with the back of my hand and dried my eyes. I looked out the window and saw my girls, now three little girls, as Ellie had joined the fun, riding bikes and tricycles, laughing and having a blast. My heart swelled.

Just about then Greer ambled up and wrapped her arms around my waist, looked up with the sweetest of grins and asked, "G-Mama, can I make some cookies?"

We walked, arms entwined, into the kitchen to whip up some of her famous cake-mix chocolate chip cookies.

And I left the Nativity just as it was.

≈

And she brought forth her firstborn son and wrapped him in swaddling clothes, and laid him in a manger . . .
Luke 2:7

RILYN'S REVELATIONS

Carly

The Grands: bottom, oldest Hayden holding youngest Isabelle, Greyson and Greer, the twins sitting middle, and Carly, Ellie, and Rilyn filling in the back

Acknowledgements

- ♥ To our grandchildren who have, each in his or her own special way, given immeasurable love and joy to Jimmy and me.

- ♥ To our children: Ginger and Chuck, Sonny and Phyllis, (and Jimmy's special crew, too) for rearing their children to love God, being compassionate toward their peers, and respectful of adults.

- ♥ To Daddy and Mama, Charles and Dara, for rearing my siblings and me in a positive home filled with Godly love.

- ♥ To Becky who has kept her foot near my behind while I wrote—(disguised as encouragement)

- ♥ To all my very, very special girlfriends.

- ♥ To Jared Evans and Gene Scott

- ♥ And especially to Rilyn—my wish is that you always share your gift of laughter and innocent observations.

About the author...

Cheryl Gore Pollard lives in rural Heard County, Georgia, with her husband, Jimmy. She is a retired educator and enjoys spending time with her seven grandchildren, writing, painting, gardening, and making pottery.

Her writing style allows the reader to merge with the characters. They are transported into their 'read,' and see and hear the characters as they tell the story. Readers recall personal memories as the story unfolds, bringing meaning and inspiration to fill the heart.

Mrs. Pollard is the international author of two books, *Fording* and *Sunrise*, and a third collaboration, *Love Lifted Me*, all found on Amazon.com

She is presently working on volume three of the trilogy, titled *Haybo*, which spans decades following her characters' lives, setting them in the Civil War desolated south.

Other Books by Cheryl Gore Pollard

Fording, Volume 1

Sunrise Volume 2

AND

Love Lifted Me, collaboration

**Coming soon: Haybo Volume 3

www.ingramcontent.com/pod-product-compliance
Lightning Source LLC
Chambersburg PA
CBHW041806160426
43202CB00001B/2